# Life Expressed in 25 Words or Less

12/24/16

Milt & Edie —
Enjoy the journey!
Merry Christmas,
Jack

Happy Anniversary Too!

# Life Expressed in 25 Words or Less

### Distilled Wisdom for Life
### Foreword by Francis X. Ryan

## Jack Cantwell

Copyright © 2016 by Jack Cantwell.

| Library of Congress Control Number: | 2016905954 |
|---|---|
| ISBN: Hardcover | 978-1-5144-8453-1 |
| Softcover | 978-1-5144-8452-4 |
| eBook | 978-1-5144-8451-7 |

All rights reserved. No part of this book may be reproduced or transmitted in any form or by any means, electronic or mechanical, including photocopying, recording, or by any information storage and retrieval system, without permission in writing from the copyright owner.

This is a work of fiction. Names, characters, places and incidents either are the product of the author's imagination or are used fictitiously, and any resemblance to any actual persons, living or dead, events, or locales is entirely coincidental.

Any people depicted in stock imagery provided by Thinkstock are models, and such images are being used for illustrative purposes only.
Certain stock imagery © Thinkstock.

Print information available on the last page.


Rev. date: 04/25/2016



**To order additional copies of this book, contact:**
Xlibris
1-888-795-4274
www.Xlibris.com
Orders@Xlibris.com
736984

To my wife of over 55 years
and counting,
Patricia;

our three
children,
Kevin, Lisa, and Monica,

and our seven grandchildren
(oldest to youngest)
Kyle, Jack, Meagan, Aidan, Molly, Theo, and Elana

---

**God is good.**

Love

# Foreword

Throughout life, particularly as one gets older, one begins to reflect—on life, relationships, random events, and the meaning of it all.

Jack Cantwell has in 25 words or less, with each one of his haiku's, provided ample opportunity for the reader to reminisce about wonderful events in your own life. The thoughts expressed in so few words have such profound meaning and impact that hours, perhaps days, perhaps weeks later you will experience something in your own life that gives you an "A Ha" reflection on the wisdom of Jack's words.

The stories behind the haiku give you a warm insight into the man who authored this ingenious life's reflection. The stories give you a frame of reference that propels you into the middle of the haiku and into Jack's life. The haiku then becomes part of you because you have become part of Haiku and Jack's own experiences.

As you read each reflection you will think back on moments in your own life when you have experienced similar life's events.

Most of the haiku's inspired me but one in particular impacted me greatly because of my own life's experiences which Jack allowed me to contemplate, internalize, and remember with fondness.

"**Shapeless**
Yet it shapes our lives.
A **gift** from God.
Compassion.

shape-
less
dream

She **dreamt** she was awake.
So was it really a **dream?**"

The haiku reminded me of the compassion that was shown to me when I was trying to complete a walk across America for children with disabilities. I was exhausted. I had completed almost 1450 miles of a journey of 2806 miles across the nation. I had injured my ankle about 800 miles earlier and was in extreme discomfort. I thought about quitting the walk. So I decided to have breakfast, call my family, and had considered calling it a day. But then a young teenage waitress at the truck stop where I ate uttered these words to the then 63 year old walker, "you have to have faith". When I told her that I did have faith she replied that she could see in my eyes that I was beaten even know I was outwardly bubbly to the crowd. She was right. Her compassion towards me at that moment and her wisdom of seeing beyond the outward me were the compassion I needed to remind me to have compassion for our children and to complete my journey. Jack's haiku reminded me that she was, in reality, a messenger from God.

You see with each "Life Expressed in 25 Words or Less" Jack Cantwell will bring to you his life experience and wisdom, the beautiful stories behind them, and the bridge for you so that his haiku becomes your "A Ha" moment.

Jack has magnificently brought the reader into his stories, his life, his wisdom and his genius and then somehow magically at the end those stories become yours. The connection you will feel with Jack, his stories, and his life will bring warmth and tranquility to your day that will live well beyond the reading of the book.

I am reminded in reading Jack's book that my walk across America and his coverage of my walk is what brought me into Jack's haiku world. I thought of the irony of having to walk 2806 miles to meet someone who only lived 5 miles away from me to begin a friendship that will last a lifetime. Jack gave me my own personal haiku moment- A HA!

Francis X. Ryan, KM, CPA, COLONEL, USMCR (RET.)

# Introduction

My name is Jack Cantwell. By day I do paid marketing for clients and pro bono marketing work for select charities and my church St. Mary's, Lebanon, Pa.

By night I work at becoming a published author, when I'm not teaching a marketing or sales class for Elizabethtown College

I had this idea when my wife Pat and I lived in Japan from 1987 to 1991.

If I observe things and think thoughts, can they be expressed in random word pictures? That's the concept of haiku isn't it? Can each thought be expressed in 25 words or less? Pure haiku is 17 syllables (too difficult for me), so I created my own rule of 25 words or less.

I tried it out. Each first attempt uses more than 25 words. The editing is part of the challenge and the fun.

The next step was easy to decide. Like a good marketing guy, I wrote a "sample" book, had 150 copies printed and gave them away to friends, relatives, business colleagues and people who heard about it and asked for a copy.

In return I asked for feedback.

The results were highly encouraging, which motivated me to take this project to the next level. This is what you're reading now. The original work is still included, Plus, this introduction is longer; there are many new word-pictures, more than double the entries in the original "sample" book. And in response to requests following an interview on a radio talk show, I wrote a new section of Backstories.

Thank you in advance for climbing aboard. Some of my "sample" readers called this "poetry for the non-poetry reader"; others observed that they were reading my autobiography "in small bites".

Remarks like that are woven into the motivation to keep going with the book. God has blessed me with a good life, and I'm pleased to open the door and invite you to be part of it through this medium, the Haiku-inspired word pictures. The "life" connection has also inspired the title of the book.

Before we go further, here is a sampling of the feedback (Do these qualify as "reviews"?). Maybe they'll give you some reading tips going forward:

- "I loved it. Very creative book"—Debbie B., PR Professional
- "I first visualized the picture you were creating, even though I have not been to Japan. Then a few minutes later I visualized a scene from my past. I found it all so relaxing and enjoyable"—Dick B. Retired radio broadcaster
- "I have never seen anything quite like it. My wife and I read it carefully and enjoyed it"—Dave W., Sports information Professional
- "In its simplicity, the collection demonstrates a depth of spirit and wonder."—Susan O., Professional Journalist
- "It was very special. My wife is also enjoying it" Jerry G., Retired Executive
- "I enjoyed your haiku-inspired A Ha Moments. Rita says "thank you" 'cause I don't read much poetry" Allen F., Network TV Producer
- "I am enjoying the book you sent me. The haikus definitely paint scenes and emotions"—Brett D. Graphic Artist
- "Offers food for thought and is not a "speed read"—Esther H., Family Therapist
- "I didn't understand it Daddy"—Jack H., age 7
- "My husband and I loved the book. We laughed out loud at some (crinkle, crinkle) and felt sad at others. I really liked envisioning what you "painted" for us."—Tanya W., International Charity Executive Director

- "I LOVED it. I'm not sure which my favorite is. I've read it twice and keep changing my mind" - Joan K., Psychologist
- "I love it so much I had my 14 and 16 year old daughters read it. We talked about it over dinner. It created meaningful family discussion" Kirk H., College Management Executive
- "Sat down with a glass of wine and immersed myself in the book. Content and layout well done. Great job"—George C., Retired Government Safety Officer
- "Word efficiency is such a vital idea. Wonderful use of strong verbs in the book"—Jennifer H., Freelance Writer
- "It is beautifully done and speaks to the essence of so many things. I love the combination of personal experience and world events. I got the "picture" as I journey through the book"—Kim K. U—Health Services Company CEO
- "Great book. I truly enjoyed reading it and reflecting on many of your moments. It made me think about similar moments in my life"—Tom B., Retired College Dean of Communications
- "Distilled Wisdom for Life."– Tom R. College President
- "A niche offering, but a worthwhile niche. Absolutely, there are people who would pay good money for this book" Terry M., Advertising Professional
- "I am enjoying your sublime A Ha Moments. My favorite: brisk walk in Yoyogi Park" - Eric R., College Executive
- "The collection was a glimpse into an interesting mind. A few of the images evoked made me chuckle out loud. A very pleasurable read"—Gordon W. Radio News Reporter
- "Jack you have found your calling"—Mark M, Award winning advertising writer.
- "I like these entries Jack. Tell me the stories behind them" Laura L., Radio Talk Show Host

Thanks to everyone who took the time to read the "sample" book, and especially to take the time to provide such positive feedback. You made the decision to publish very clear.

# A message from Jack Cantwell

Hi—Welcome to my world of word pictures. They represent selected random thoughts that span my entire life. But the original inspiration for the book started during the late 1980's when I was living and working in Japan. At the time I became intrigued by the concept of haiku (described in the Preface). Here's a reading tip for maximum enjoyment:

1. Read the prologue for background
2. Read the first word picture.
3. Pause
4. Read the next one.
5. Pause
6. Keep repeating the process

I hope you "get the picture" as you read.

Some of my "American haikus" are written for humor. Some are simple observations of life experiences. Some are mere thoughts, or expressions of faith. Every entry relates to my life in some way.

Thanks in advance for taking the time to read. I would appreciate feedback too. This will help me determine if this book has life beyond this publication. The marketing guy in me is looking for "test results". You can reach me by email (jack@skylimitmarketing.com), phone

(717-269-0288) or visit my business website (www.skylimitmarketing.com)

Special thanks to Kenn Kreiser (Kenn Kreiser Design, Annville, Pa) for the wonderful graphic treatment; and to Mary Kohler and her team of professionals at H&H Graphics in Lancaster, Pa for the quality printing of the original book.

Thanks also:

1. To Charisse, Nicole, Richard and the Xlibris team for helping me bring "Life Expressed in 25 Words or Less" to life.
2. To my friend Ithaca College President Tom Rochon. He sent me a testimonial that inspired the subtitle ("Distilled Wisdom for Life")
3. To talented artist MJ McFalls—the Seagull Air War haiku inspired her to turn the episode into an art rendering.
4. To my friend Frank Ryan—who led me to Xlibris. They are his publisher as well. I was honored when he agreed to write the Foreword.
5. To all the friends, family, and business colleagues, who encouraged me to keep writing after the original sample book, and to get this project done.
6. To God, for a blessed life, good health, and a brain that is still in good working order. I'm probably not the oldest first time author in America—but I think I'm in the top tier☺.

One of my life's blessings is crossing paths with people like you. This book is just another tool to make it happen.

Best wishes for a healthy and happy rest of 2016 and beyond.

Writing word pictures is challenging and fun.

Try it yourself ☺

Jack

**M**y life's journey landed me in Japan for a wonderful five-year career experience from 1987 until 1991.

It was there that I discovered a poetic style called haiku, a technique that fascinated me because the writer challenged himself or herself to express a moment in time in just seventeen syllables. Each haiku is a word picture, frozen in time.

I've devoted a portion of my professional life to writing marketing- and advertising-related things—everything from ads, commercials, website texts, press releases, brochures, postcards, billboards, company profiles, and feel-good community news stories.

The best writing I've done has something in common—word efficiency. Say what you have to say clearly and succinctly. Unnecessary words or redundancies are a waste of the reader's time. Most importantly, the intended message can get muddy and unclear.

Enter the concept and spirit of haiku. Say what you have to say without wasted words.

Since this is my version of the concept, I've made up my own ground rule—express a clear "word pictures" in twenty-five words or less. I find this exercise is good practice for the writing I do professionally. Assignments have restrictions like timing for broadcast pieces or word count limits for certain PR tasks.

The practice of writing my haiku-inspired word pictures helps me become a better writer in general. Find the words that express the intended message best.

I'm sharing my random aha moments in the pages that follow. I hope you get the picture(s) as you take your own journey. Enjoy!

# Preface

# part 1

The Japan
and
Southeast Asia
Years

Dream

**Morning** Tokyo rush.
Subway trains regurgitate
endless bobbleheaded commuters.
Heads in **motion** create a black sea.

# morning
# rush

8:55 a.m.
A sea of black-haired **workers**
run to beat the time clock.
An office lady loses
her shoe in the **rush**.

**Standing** at the Harajuku trestle seeing faces in the passing train. How many see **back**?

# standing worlds

Bullet train passengers
sit **side by side**.
Sleeper.
Reader.
Daydreamer.
Traveling in the same direction.
Living in different **worlds**.

Rice fields in China.
Water buffalo–driven plows toil away.
A **time** that was
is still
a time that **is**.

# time
# aloft

Clash of the ages.
The bus **rolls** over the water buffalo.
Wheels **aloft**. Legs to the sky.
South China traffic jam.

Two sisters reunite
on the Shinjuku Station platform.
The waggy-tailed dog
feels the **joy**
with **perpetual** lickamotion.

# joy
# boredom

A limo bus plods
to Narita airport.
Creeping **traffic**
in pouring rain.
Ultimate **boredom**.

Brisk walk in Yoyogi Park.
**Think**.
Observe.
Plan.
Mind sharper. Body **stronger**.
Good decision.

# think
# thoughts

**Sunlit** morning.
Yoyogi Park.
The man contemplates
the artificial lake
and conjures up real **thoughts**

She perches on top of the bench
**looking** over the back.
He squats in the grass
looking up at her.
They are communicative
and **comfortable**.

# looking
# demure

The **demure** Japanese elevator girl
announces the floor to the wall,
hoping you get the **message**.

The **smiling** Japanese waitress
hearing footsteps
bellows a welcome **greeting**
to no one in particular.

# smiling
# sparrows

Three **dark** objects float lightly
and settle on the moist pavement.
What appears to be autumn leaves
are really **sparrows**.

Hundreds of Chinese laborers wielding hand tools only, **level** an enormous **field** to build a new airport. Labor trumps technology.

# level
# stars

Brightest **stars**.
Clearest night.
Bali mountain.
Center **stage**.

The clouds part. I stand **frozen** at what I see. Nothing unfolds quite like **Mount Fuji**.

# clouds
# unfold

Sukiyaki Dinner.
Beautifully presented.
Japan newcomer picks up and swallows
Green paste-like garnish.
Breathless discovery of **wasabi** mustard.
Whoa boy!

# Wasabi rice

Madame Tatsumi stirs her
famous fried **rice**
while nursing her baby.
Her customers don't care.
The fried rice is *that* good!

Life Expressed in 25 Words or Less

44th floor happening.
Strange **dizzy** spell feeling.
Look. Everyone is freeze-
frame motionless.
Building finally stops swaying.
Office people resume normal work.
Another Japan **earthquake** passes.

# Dizzy earthquake

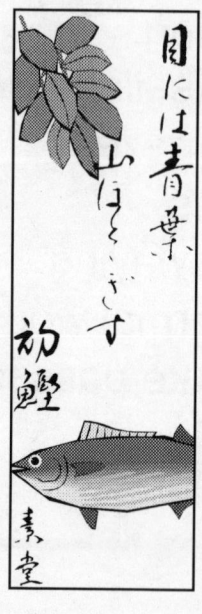 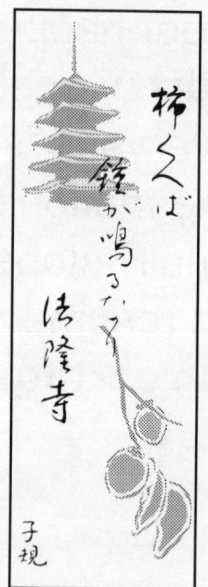 

Happiness

Other Places
Other Years
Humor, Faith,
and Other
Thoughts

Peace

Going to **church**
Looking for **God**
and surprise,
finding myself.

# God
# faith

The lonely soldier
before deployment
finds a church.
He feels a silent **voice** say
When you get there
I will be there too.
**Faith** replaces fear.

painting by M.J. McFalls

*Don't Stop Even! Love you so much ♡ Mary*

Life Expressed in 25 Words or Less

The pelican squadron
**negotiates** the skies
above the California **coastline**.
Fish beware.

# negotiates
# war

Conflict in the skies.
The **food** is mine!
Squawk.
I want it.
Seagull air **war**.

**Shapeless**.
Yet it shapes our lives.
A **gift** from God.
Compassion.

# shape-
# less
# dream

She **dreamt** she was awake.
So was it really a **dream**?

Fishing in the Everglades.
Gray sky.
Gray water.
No **horizon**.
Blank gray canvas.
**Peace**.

# peace
# God

Tree branches dance
in the whistling wind.
**God** makes music
in the **tranquility**
of a retreat at Malvern.

I am eleven thousand feet tall.
When I **grow** up
I want to **inspire**
just like Mount Fuji.
Sincerely, Mount Hood

# inspire
# goals

Now that **goals**
have been **achieved**.
He asks,
Who am I?

Green mountains **reflected**
in the pond
rippled by ducks.
**Scene** seen from the train.

# reflected feeling

Full moon.
The **feeling** returns.
I cannot help **myself**.
Ahhhhhhoooooooohh!

Wagons in the yard.
Horses graze.
A team of men in **straw hats**
turn pieces of lumber
into an Amish barn.

# amish patch-work

Flight UA90 drifts
over California farmland.
A patchwork quilt is
bathed in the **summer sun**.

Sheep **run** in circles
as **fast** as they can
along the Scottish meadow fence.
Sheeplechase.

# run
# already

**Hey**, *Wheel of Fortune* is on.
*Jeopardy* is next.
**Wait** a minute. Can it be?
Am I a senior citizen already?

Get things in order.
Sit in the sun.
Cheer for old Notre Dame.
A special man **celebrates**
the twilight of his **life**.
Dear departed Uncle George.

# life

# search

**Soulful** brown eyes gaze upward.
The tiny tot begs.
Her little hands
touch the tourist grandmother
in **search** of a better life.
Tijuana heartbreak.

Tab pull.
Whoosh.
**Drink**.
**Crush**.
Macho can toss.
Miller time is history.

# crush
# crinkle

Crinkle, crinkle
little car.
Next stop?
**Body shop**.

The 100 mph tailgater
swerves me **right**
and laughs maniacally
from his silver car.
The face of the devil
etched in my **mind**.
Forever.

# mind
# control

Car loses **control**
on a three-lane highway.
Skids west across northbound lanes.
Stops unharmed in the left shoulder.
Highway **miracle**.
No other explanation.

Red Sox make **history**
from 3 down to 4 win joy.
Yankees go home
with the curse in tow.
Bambino **rests** at last.

# history
# rests

Madness
In a pressure cooker explosion.
Joy becomes Sorrow.
Elation. Shock.
Laughter. Tears.
Marathon **innocence**
**Forever lost** in Boston.

# forever lost

Obstruction. Sad.
Pick off. Happy.
World Series game endings in St. Louis.
Two **bizzare**.
Red Sox history enriched.

# Bizzare
# Strong

Three angels smile down approvingly
as 36000 marathoners
grind out 26.2 miles,
running in 2014 with one single focus:
Boston will always be **strong**.

Meow at the water dish,
Cat-speak for "I'm thirsty".
Meow at the food dish,
**Cat-speak** for something different.
Look it up.

# Cat-speak Sandpaper

7 am.
Head butt to bicep.
**Sandpaper** lick on forearm.
Furry alarm cat does his thing.

November 22, 1963. 1 PM. Buffalo, NY.
President **Kennedy** has been
shot says the radio news.
Eddie the barber stops
trimming his customer.
Where were you?

# Kennedy
# Newtown

A brave **Newtown** mother
Copes with the loss of her slain
little daughter, with fervent belief
that the Good Shepherd cares for her
precious lamb.

Don't cry Ya Ya
**Santa** will bring you one for Christmas.
Big brother 3, consoles sister 2,
during a potty training demonstration.

# Santa
# Santa

Dear **Santa**,
Enjoy the milk and cookies.
P.S. I drank some of the milk
'cause I was needing a drink.
Full disclosure at age 7.

Computers come with
Built-in knowledge
and information.
**Wisdom** not included.

# Wisdom Milestones

Now that **milestones** have been reached,
He pauses and asks
Who am I now?
And where do I go next?

Two **cars** at stoplight.
Windows rolled down.
Angry stare from left.
You almost hit us.
Sorry, didn't see you.
Honest reply does not quell anger.

# Cars Driving

Night **driving**. Dark narrow road.
Something black and white appears.
Thud. Road kill.
Unmistakable lingering odor
transforms the vehicle
Into a 1999 Skunk-mobile

**Born** 5 weeks early.
Dodges every medical bullet.
At 10 he scores a soccer goal
In front of joyful grandparents.
Icing on God's miracle cake.

# Born
# Boy

Son calls Parents.
It's a **boy**.
Instant realization.
Our son has a son of his own.
Once-in-a-lifetime stunning moment.
Speechless.

**Illiterate** man works hard
To learn reading,
So he can sing karaoke.
Motivation is a good thing,
whatever the reason.

# Illiterate Homeless

The **homeless** man empties his pockets
And gives his $10.46
to another man walking for
a children's charity.
Compassion has nothing to
do with economics.

There're out there.
Heard but not seen.
Venting. Sharing. Listening.
Same time. Same station.
The **Talk** Radio stage is set.

# Talk

# Like

First word of every teen sentence.
Facebook scorecard word.
The culture of LIKE is here to stay,
**Like** it or not.

A **Midnight** Star illuminates
a Bethlehem stable.
Three Wise Men drawn to the light.
*Their* lives, *all* lives thereafter
Changed by Who was there.

# Midnight Garden

I look out the window of
my spare Malvern Retreat room.
There it is, the Pieta in the **garden**.
I love a room with a view.

Career-building job **changes**,
All on St. Patrick's Day.
1960. 1962. 1969. 1971. 1974.
1978. 1987. 1995. 1997.1999.
Luck of the Irish is real.

# Changes
# Excites

So many roads traveled
Yet the one ahead still **excites**.
He feels truly blessed with life.

Family **fun** gift under the tree.
A sealed bag of monkey breath.
A game of rock paper scissors
determines who opens it.

# Fun Song

Original birthday **song** for daughter
By her 8-year old daughter
Lyrics include
I'm glad I'm an ice cube
in your cup of life.

**Silent** weekend retreat.
A crucifix on my desk as I write,
contemplating the **magnitude**
Of the most self-sacrificing
act known to man.
Indescribable feeling.

# Silent
# Magnitude

Excuse me Sir.
Are you aware that your
bird-feeder is empty?
Talking **squirrel** cartoon
makes me chuckle.

# Squirrel
# Redfish

The reluctant **redfish**
is hauled into the kayak.
Fighting and squirming action
capsizes the kayak
and sets the redfish free.

Pre-arranged.
The good neighbor deposits
a cock-a-poo puppy
In our empty kitchen.
The weekend away ends
in pure family joy.
Daughter's **dream** comes true.

# Dream
# Sleep

Sobbing uncontrollably
as my morning jogging pal is put to **sleep**.
How can the loss of a little dog
unleash so much emotion?

Ebbets Field, **Brooklyn**.
First time experience
For a 6 year old Dodgers fan.
Dodgers 5 Braves 0.
Thanks Grandpa and Kirbe Higbe.

# Brooklyn Dodger

Handmade PBJ in hand,
7 year-old boy enthusiastically walks
to a Brooklyn **Dodger** game by himself.
This outing would shock parents today,
but not in 1941.

A tour of Staten Island garbage dumps
In a chauffeur-driven limousine.
A day in the life of
the Commissioner of
Sanitation's **grandson**.

# Grandson
# Brother

Bowling-ball shaped Franciscan **Brother**
Winds up and paddles an
out-of-line 5$^{th}$ grader.
The sting of Brother Teddy's
Board of Education
lingers in the lifetime memory bank.

Supremely peaceful on
the beach at dusk.
Crashing waves provide the
background noise.
A soft breeze and screeching
**seagulls** overhead
fill in the rhythm section.

# Seagulls
# Birds

Perched on a tree branch
surrounded by peers.
Staring ahead. Confused. Silent.
Life on a snow-filled day is for the **birds**.
Not!

Neck stretching **forward.**
Feet scrambling to **catch** up.
The chicken crosses the road. Why?

# catch
# dream

He had a **dream**.
He gave it a deadline.
It became a **goal**.

Daughter's golden lab named **Moose**
Photographed chest deep
in the snow.
Pleased to spot my first snow moose
of the winter.

# Moose Bat

A **bat** falls from a tree
into the lap of a man in a
parked convertible.
The crotch-scratching bat
causes the man to
vault from the convertible
in world record time.

An Amish **buggy**
clip clops along in front of me.
Pleasantly enduring a
Pennsylvania Dutch Country version
of a traffic slowdown.

# Buggy Horses

Bathed in the October sun,
two golden-hued **horses**
stand like statues in the dewy meadow.
A special sight for sore or any eyes.

Two tips for a lasting marriage.
Spouse before self.
Shared faith in **God**.
Working for over 55 years so far.

# God

# Serve

He awoke with a question in his head.
Why am I here?
Short answer,
To **serve**.

In the name of the Father
the Son
And the Holy **Spirit**.
Good words to begin all things.

# Spirit
# Yours

My friend Father Ed's favorite prayer.
I can't.
You must.
I'm **yours**.
Show me the way.

Even at age 80, the son
senses the presence
of his dear **departed** mother
on Mother's Day.
Feeling the love from above
never gets old.

# Departed Grief

Beloved Son, 36, precedes
his parents in death.
This writer discovers there are no words
that can express the depth
of parental **grief**.

Two twin girls
Decked out in **pure** white dresses
Receive holy communion
for the first time.
Instant bond with Jesus.
Guaranteed friends for life.

# Pure
# Forever

Anticipate.
Experience.
Remember.
Life's special times are **forever**.

Reach out and clutch your
college **diploma**
With a handshake and
background applause.
Hey wait!
The adult me has just emerged.
I'm ready.

# Diploma Ponder

One word solution to replace
a short-fused reaction
to a verbal attack.
The word is **PONDER**.

He looked beneath his feet
and noticed **grass** growing.
I'm shocked, he said,
This should not be happening.

# Grass

# Spring

Wintery weather continues
as the official first day of **spring**
is noted on the calendar.
Arriving robins perfect
the art of the frown

**Wet** sand sucks the heat
out of his hands
as he pushes them beneath
the shoreline surface
Granules gently soften the skin.
Peace prevails

# Wet Squiggly

**Squiggly** worms occupy the
moist blacktop driveway.
Spring has arrived.
Flying creatures alerted that
The Early Bird Buffet is
open for business.

The tyrannical King orders the
Saddest Easter Bunny,
Come back after lunch so
you can be beheaded.
Six year old writer rocks
her **imagination**.

# Imagination
# Wonderful

Older Actor delivers his interpretation
of the classic character
Clarence the Angel,
to the delight of another
appreciative audience.
Indeed It *is* a **Wonderful** Life.

Triumphant **Optimist** shouts,
Another Mountain scaled.
Keep those Molehills coming!

# Optimist Bonding

He listens to gossip and
shakes his head.
To some it becomes a form
of personal **bonding**.
But in reality gossip is a cancer
with no known cure.

Bare branches adorn the
top of a leaf-filled tree.
The sight evokes a picture
of an **Indian** in profile,
showing off his fresh Mohawk haircut.

# Indian

# Amish

Laundered shirts flap in the breeze
On the **Amish** Farm clothesline.
Want to save more energy?
Learn stuff from the Amish.

Humane Society staffer hands cat to Pat.
Purring connection seals the deal.
Rescued calico **kitten** has a new home.
God orchestrates another
win-win scenario.

# Kitten Steals

Woman prepares green beans
with the pot on her lap.
Playful kitten **steals** a
bean and dashes off.
Family bean stalker strikes again.

Father **scolds** son and takes
his eyes off the road.
The on-horse power Amish
buggy clops along,
Unaware of the danger behind.

# Scolds

# Slap

Broken car door handle.
Inside opening impossible.
Help recruited to open door from outside.
Finally, Light bulb moment.
Forehead **slap**.
Roll the window down Jack!

Archbishop of Los Angeles.
MLB GM.
Palace **Vaudeville** Performer.
Staten Island Commissioner of Sanitation.
Many self-made men.
Many women of faith.
What's in your DNA?

# Vaudeville Baby

Denture-making professional
fits his **baby** boy with a
perfect set of teeth.
Smiling baby causes shock and amusement
at family and other social gatherings.

# part 3

## The Backstories

And now, in the words of the late Paul Harvey (one of the great radio voices ever), it's time for *"the rest of the story."*

I was blessed with very positive feedback to the original printing of my word pictures, from a wide variety of readers.

Thank you, dear readers. You inspired me to take the work to this next level.

I'd also be pleased to get more feedback about this work. I've heard varying descriptions ranging from "Pictures that I can see too" to "Some of them reminded me of my own life" to "Never read anything like this" to "I don't read poetry but this was different" to "Like reading your autobiography in random bite-size portions." Bottom line—I hope you felt it was worth your time and that you learned something new.

The feedback includes requests for some backstories—the actual incidents that inspired the work you have just read. This idea crystallized when I appeared on a local radio talk show. The host, Laura Le Beau, read some of her favorites, and I shared the background story for each one she chose. It was a fun and interesting experience. I've thought it over and decided that sharing some background stories should also be part of the book.

So here we go.

As I mentioned in the preface, the inspiration to adapt the concept of haiku into my own word pictures began while I was enjoying a great five-year period of my career, based in Tokyo from 1987 until 1991. It included extensive travel and work experiences throughout the Far East.

Subsequently I examined my whole life experience and looked for special moments that led to word picture expression. They range from my childhood in Brooklyn, New York, to present day Lebanon, Pennsylvania, and everywhere in between. "Everywhere" includes Brooklyn; Pittsburgh; Newburgh, New York; Joliet, Illinois; Lancaster, Pennsylvania; army years in Fort Jackson, South Carolina; Fort Devins, Massachusetts; Army Language School (Korean) Monterey, California; Tokyo (Far East HQ for Army Security Agency), Seoul, and Yong Dong Po, Korea; then back to Tokyo.

Civilian life resumed in Ithaca, New York (Ithaca College), and Lebanon, Pennsylvania (the first time for first job at WLYH-TV). Lebanon is also where I met my wife, Pat, on a blind date (she was with the other guy), then career moves to Buffalo, Boston, Tokyo (to run a marketing office—who knew I would get back to Japan?), London, Chicago, Toronto, Charlotte, San Diego, then back to Lebanon to stay in 1999. The career circle from and then back to Lebanon, took almost thirty-nine years, with never a dull moment.

The first "American haiku" inspiration happened in suburban Tokyo on a dark, misty, rainy night. I was walking down a quiet street and spotted a tree ahead of me, which seemed to be shedding leaves onto the moist pavement. As I got closer I realized that they were not leaves, but a group of sparrows descending slowly to the ground. Wow, what a nice surprise.

I took a scrap of paper from my pocket and wrote a word picture of what I had just witnessed—and my haiku-inspired writing passion was born.

Usually when I get inspired by a moment, I just write and describe the thought that popped in my head or the scene I just observed. Most of the time, the first draft involves more than twenty-five words. The challenge is then to edit the text and get rid of the fat. The real satisfaction is in the fun of making the words as efficient and descriptive as they can be within the guidelines.

Compare this thought process to the theory of brainstorming—no editing, just letting the mind flow. When this is done, keep editing until the final picture emerges clearly.

Many of the thoughts expressed in the book are just that, thoughts and ideas. There is no backstory for these moments, just the voice of life experience at work.

But there are also many "aha moments" that are inspired by unforgettable events in my life. I'm pleased to share some of these stories here, in no particular chronological order. If you have questions about any word picture not covered, just ask. That's what friends are for.

# Highway Miracle

I was teaching a marketing class in Harrisburg on a cold February night in 2010. Class ran from 6:00 p.m. to 10:00 p.m. The weather was okay when I arrived, but at 10:00 p.m. things had changed for the worse. There was a wet snow falling, with below-freezing temperatures. Driving conditions were just plain awful.

To add to the excitement, my 1996 Mercedes was not ready for the road conditions. It had rear-wheel drive, an empty trunk, and tires that had barely passed inspection.

I drove slowly down North Front Street, heading for Highway I-83. If I attempted to pick up speed, I could feel the rear end sway. Steady as she goes, I think.

The real problem occurred when I reached the entrance ramp to I-83, heading north toward Hershey. I could see three lanes of traffic, cars and trucks, moving at slightly below normal speed. A retaining wall separated the north and southbound traffic.

The instant I reached the top of the ramp and picked up speed, I completely lost control of the car. Traffic was heading north while the Mercedes traveled due west, heading directly toward the wall. I remember being calm, like I was playing a role in a slow-motion movie. I played with the steering wheel but had no control over it. *I'm going to hit the wall*, I thought. A feeling of calm swept over me. I was convinced that *this was it!* The wall was in the sight of my hood ornament.

And then . . . like a film cutting to the next scene, the car was stopped, parallel to the wall, facing north, in an undersized breakdown lane.

I had *not hit the wall*.

*My car was not hit by a northbound car or truck.*

What the heck just happened? I couldn't move. I sat there stunned, until I turned on the blinkers. I maneuvered the car slowly to the far-right lane and kept the speed at about twenty miles per hour. Cars were passing me all the way.

There were a couple of other uneasy moments, as my normal forty-five-minute drive took a little over two hours. I arrived home. No damage to the car and no physical damage to myself. The emotional scars will always be there.

I continued to drive the car, but with three hundred pounds of salt and sand in the trunk from November through March each year. I invested in good tires the day after the incident and made sure they didn't get worn to the extent of that all-too-memorable night.

Shortly after the incident, I told the story to a friend of mine, an elderly Jesuit priest, Father Ed Sanders. He told me, "Jack, you experienced a miracle. Every day from now on is a gift."

I now try to live my life with this philosophy, and I think I'm a better person as a result.

In a strange way, the highway miracle has been good for me. But I'm not craving a repeat performance ever again. Drive safely, everyone!

*Lifestyle update.* My wife and I eventually determined that we only needed one car (she doesn't like driving anymore), so the Mercedes was sold to a nice local couple after sixteen years of ownership, including one night behind the wheel that will never be forgotten.

# Madame Tatsumi's Famous Fried Rice

Following completion of my Korean language training at the Army Language School in Monterey, California, I was sent first to Tokyo to learn my job as a communications intelligence specialist, then for a tour of duty in Korea to apply my learning, then back to Far East headquarters to teach the new guys what to do before they were sent to Korea. It was a great experience! During my second stint (as a teacher) I won Soldier of the Week, which earned me a twenty-four-hour pass when I was not on duty.

I took advantage of the free time and got involved in the Tokyo Amateur Dramatic Club (TADC), the only live Western theater productions that put on plays in English. Our productions were staged at the Imperial Hotel in Tokyo, and reviewed by professional critics. The acting troupe was a mix of amateurs and professionals. I appeared as Peter the boyfriend in the TADC production of *The Diary of Anne Frank* at the same time it was running on Broadway. We had meetings and social gatherings at the Dutch Embassy. The TADC head was the Netherlands ambassador to Japan. Life was good.

My free pass status allowed me to go off base from time to time to enjoy Japanese fried rice and local beer at a little neighborhood restaurant called Madame Tatsumi's. The place had a counter and about six or eight stools. That was it! I still remember, almost every time I went there, Madame Tatsumi, the only person working there, would be stirring a big wok of her product with one hand, while she held her nursing baby with the other. The two were one.

No one really cared or paid attention. All we knew was her fried rice was to die for.

I also devoted part of my schedule to sports writing. I covered post sports for our newspaper and contributed articles on our basketball team (almost NBA quality) to the *Stars and Stripes* newspaper circulated all over Japan. I was also a player—got pretty good at softball and Ping-Pong.

The army tried to persuade me to sign up for OCS (officer candidate school), but I chose to leave the service after my three-year enlistment and go on to Ithaca College to complete my education. In retrospect, I chose the right path.

# Deployed Soldier

I had earned a top secret security clearance and completed my training in Korean language at the Presidio of Monterey Language School in California.

My short home leave was finished. Now it was time to report to Fort Washington near Seattle to be processed and board a troop ship for a two-week journey to Yokohama, Japan, to start more training at the Far East headquarters of the army security agency in nearby Tokyo.

The trip began as I boarded a flight from New York to Seattle on United Airlines in early March 1955. I had the good fortune to volunteer to be bumped from an overbooked earlier flight, so I had a first-class seat and some extra cash, enough for a hotel room when I landed in Seattle a day ahead of reporting time to Fort Washington.

This was my first long journey away from home and family. In the days leading up to my departure, I suffered attacks of anxiety. I woke up every night, gasping for breath. I don't recall ever being so nervous about anything in my life.

After a smooth and comfortable flight, which included being fussed over by a beautiful red-haired United Airlines stewardess, I arrived in Seattle and found an affordable hotel room.

I had an afternoon and evening to kill, so I took a leisurely stroll around the neighborhood. Try as I might, I couldn't shake the feeling of apprehension.

As if I was led to it, I stopped in front of a Catholic church. *Perhaps a visit would help*, I thought. And into the church I went.

After a few minutes of kneeling in silent prayer, a strange, peaceful feeling swept over me. I was filled with feelings of peace and relaxation. A thought popped into my head. It was like an inner voice that said *Hey, Jack, you need not be so afraid. Remember, wherever you are, I am there too.* Wow.

I don't know how else to describe it, but when I left that church, the sense of calm continued. Faith had replaced fear, and I now faced the immediate future with a renewed sense of excitement.

I was rewarded with a two-year maturing experience, first in Japan (to be trained); then to Seoul and Yong Dong Po, Korea (to apply my training); and then, nine months later, reassigned back to Japan, where I had my first experience as a teacher, which continued for another year and a half.

My life was touched years later when a new job brought me back to Japan for a five-year assignment running a marketing office. My earlier hands-on experience with the country and the culture played an important role in getting this job.

Today, I also teach marketing and sales for Elizabethtown College. I can thank my teaching experience in Japan for helping me determine I would be good at teaching.

Connections in my life journey showed me that early experiences can pay dividends later on in life, especially when faith in God is in the mix.

# The Face of the Devil

If my wife wasn't there to witness this with me, people would say I was nuts.

We were driving to Massachusetts from Pennsylvania. I was behind the wheel. The car was cruising at a bit over seventy miles per hour, eastbound on I-78. I was in the passing lane, slowly pulling ahead of another car on the right.

All of a sudden, I looked in the rearview mirror and spotted another car behind me, driving at an unbelievable rate of speed.

I hit the accelerator as hard as I could to make sure I cleared the car in the right lane. By now the car behind me was literally riding my trunk and not slowing down!

I swerved right so fast I almost lost control of my car. The car in the left lane was now parallel with us, driving at identical speed.

My wife and I both glanced left and made eye contact with the other driver. He had starkly white hair and bright yellow eyes. There appeared to be a glow framing his face from behind.

What was the most vivid memory? His head thrown back, he laughed at us maniacally. Frightening!

After he was sure he accomplished his mission, he accelerated and burst ahead. Within seconds he was out of sight.

My wife and I looked at each other and said, simultaneously, "That was the devil!"

I'm glad she was with me because, like I said, you would think I was crazy.

This guy literally scared the hell out of us, no pun intended.

# Growing Up in Brooklyn

I've been blessed to benefit from lots of education, but the foundation of growing up as a Brooklyn street kid in the 1930s and 1940s tops the list for learning how to get through life, while keeping your head on straight and your feet on the ground.

That period of my life inspired some aha moments (stolen tricycle, Brooklyn Dodgers, garbage dump tours with Grandpa, etc.), but the actual experience of living in that environment warrants some extra attention here. I learned and lived values that are still with me. Check out words like *independence*, *street-smart*, *self-confidence*, and—from my days as a Brooklyn Eagle paperboy starting at age eleven—*entrepreneurship*, *money management*, *new business development*, and *customer service*.

I acquired a love of the game of baseball by the time I was six years old, long before Little League. My buddies and I played on vacant lots amid rock and broken glass. The balls were covered in black tape. It was rare to swing a bat that wasn't held together with screws. There were no parents around to micromanage us. We were just a bunch of fun-loving kids who loved fair play and competition.

The kids I hung out with were fellow parochial school students. We were taught by Franciscan brothers at Saint Rose of Lima School. They were tough on us and pushed us hard to learn. Yes, we were paddled. We accepted it as part of the learning process. No big deal. Best of all, there were no grudges and no teacher's pets. We appreciated that. Being an altar boy started a life of faith and service. After high school I stopped being an altar boy and stayed on the altar as lector. It still continues today.

The Cantwell clan was a big, local, Irish Catholic, close-knit family. We've scattered. None of us are in Brooklyn today. But we all remember and appreciate the life lessons we grew up with on the streets of Brooklyn.

I often wonder—what parent in their right minds would allow their seven-year-old son to go alone to a Major League Baseball park to see a game? But at the time, that's the way it was. And I've lived to tell the tale.

# The Significance of the Water Buffalo

China and the water buffalo are forever linked in my memory.

During my Japan and Asia years, I made regular trips to Southeast China to visit factories where McDonald's Happy Meal toys were manufactured. A member of the McDonald's Japan purchasing department would travel with me. Our mission was to make sure agreed quality standards for the toys were met, so they could be authorized to ship to Japan. There were literally millions of toys involved. They would not be shipped without client sign-off.

The water buffalo in the fields were a familiar site in our journey from Hong Kong into the factories. The lack of power equipment and technology was evident. There was so much available labor in China that the government kept technology on the back burner, so they could put a maximum number of laborers to work.

The water buffalo was a living symbol of that philosophy. For centuries, up to present time, fields are plowed by farmers driving water buffalo instead of labor-saving tractors.

Every construction site was filled with shovel-wielding laborers, with no high-tech equipment in sight. Heck, I even saw a field for a new airport being leveled entirely by hand by hundreds of shovel-wielding laborers.

The haiku about the water buffalo and the bus is one I witnessed myself on one of the factory trips. We were traveling a dirt road (very common) when traffic was brought to a complete standstill for several hours.

What happened? A bus had hit and killed a water buffalo. When we finally saw the accident scene, the bus was on top of the water buffalo, with its wheels in the air. The dead water buffalo was on its back, with legs pointed to the sky. It was truly a clash of the ages!

## The Adult Me Emerges

The inspiration for this one came on the evening of October 11, 2014. I had nominated a late friend and college classmate, Chet Curtis, for a Lifetime Achievement Award from our alma mater, Ithaca College. A good representation of my peers was there to honor Chet. His daughters Dana and Dawn were on hand to accept the award on behalf of their father. It was the last in a series of awards bestowed on alumni that night. It was a memorable evening.

To wrap it up, Ithaca College president Tom Rochon took to the podium for his closing remarks. I'm honored to say that Tom and I have become friends in the last four or five years, largely because I served on the alumni association board of directors for three of the years.

Tom's original closing remarks were very simple, something like "Thanks for coming. The band will continue to play, so stick around." But on his way to the dinner he paused and thought, *This is a special evening. We're honoring a group of alumni who have gone on to accomplish many good things in life. I have to say something to celebrate this wonderful occasion.* So Tom parked himself on a bench outside the campus center, and drafted these remarks.

> Why do a small number of landmarks in your life draw you back—your childhood home, your college, and maybe just one or two other places?
>
> It is not just sentimental attachment or a trip down memory lane, though that is certainly a part of it.
>
> You return to the places where something significant happened in your life. Your presence here this weekend says IC was not just an education that bridged you to your adult,

professional life. It was not only a place to make friends and have fun. *It was a place of transformation.* It is where you became the person you are today. When you revisit campus you have come to the place of your own origins as an adult.

This transformation was not given to you by professors or others. You identified your own goals and values here. You created yourself. Ithaca College offered the loving, stimulating, and protected environment for you to do that.

It is with that understanding that I welcome you back not just to the place where you earned your degree. I welcome you back to the place where the adult you was born. I welcome you home.

I advised Tom to have that park bench moved into his office. He does good work there.

Tom Rochon has since announced that he will resign from his position sometime in 2017. He gave Ithaca College eighteen month's notice to find a replacement. A period of racial unrest on campus no doubt played a role in his decision. It got me to think how grateful I am that my college experience was in simpler times. Friendships with classmates then are still, well over fifty years later, close friendships. We were living an inclusive life, without even knowing it.

## Two Bizarre

I think you've figured out that one of my passions is rooting for the Boston Red Sox, for better or worse. It's been mostly worse the last few years, with exceptions being 2004, 2007, and 2013, all of which brought World Series Championships to Red Sox nation.

I refer now to the 2013 series between the Sox and the Saint Louis Cardinals. Yes, Boston won, and for the first time since 1918, the final victory was clinched at home in "the cathedral," a.k.a. Fenway Park. David "Big Papi" Ortiz was unworldly, hitting an unbelievable .729 for the series and walking away with MVP honors.

What stands out to me are the strange ways that both games 3 and 4 (both in Saint Louis) ended. They were, as the haiku says, "two bizarre."

Game 3 was tied in the bottom of the ninth, when St. Louis runner Allen Craig ran into Sox third baseman Will Middlebrooks. The entanglement resulted in an umpire decision that Middlebrooks "obstructed" Craig, who was awarded home plate with the winning run!

Bizarre.

And sad for all of Sox Nation.

Now on to Game 4. The Red Sox led 4–2 in the bottom of the ninth. Speedy Cardinal runner Colton Wong was on first. The always dangerous Carlos Beltran was at the plate, facing Red Sox closer Koji Uehara. There were two outs. Wong took a big lead, hoping to steal second and get into scoring position. Uehara saw this and, uncharacteristically for him, threw the ball to first baseman Mike Napoli, who tagged the startled Wong out! Game over in bizarre fashion number 2!

The World Series triumph was sandwiched between last place finishes in 2012 and 2014. Some promising off-season moves have the fans excited about 2016.

You are reading this now and know if the optimism was justified. Baseball sometimes mirrors life as a real-life soap opera. Yes, I am still a die-hard Red Sox fan, no matter what.

# Princess, a.k.a. Mad Animal

There are few things that can match the joy in a family household than the presence of a beloved pet.

This is the story of one of them, a little black-and-white cockapoo dog named Princess. It began as a bit of a fairy tale. Our family of five—Pat, myself, and school-age children Kevin, Lisa, and Monica—lived in our own home in Natick, Massachusetts. I was the breadwinner, employed by the Arnold Worldwide advertising agency in Boston.

Monica discovered that there was a litter of cockapoos at a neighbor's house down the street. She made no secret of the fact that she wanted the runt of the litter and already had the name picked out for her. Pat and I played dumb, but behind the scenes made arrangements with the owners to make Princess part of our family. We took the kids away for a weekend getaway in Cape Cod and gave the key to our house to the neighbor, who deposited the dog in our kitchen on Sunday evening, just before we returned. I think you can imagine the scene when we returned home! Look up *pure joy* in the dictionary, and you'll find a picture of the official addition of Princess to our family.

The little dog was a wonderful family pet, especially for me. My morning routine was to get up at 5:30 a.m. and go on a three-mile neighborhood run before showering, dressing, and heading for the commuter train to Boston. I could not get out of the house without Princess bolting out with me. I would run three miles, Princess would do twelve, circling every backyard, dashing ahead, waiting for me to catch up, then dashing away again.

And then, when I would return after a somewhat stressful day (and sometimes late) at the office, the stress would melt away instantly when Princess greeted me in mad animal fashion. She was convinced five nights a week that I single-handedly won World War 3!

The downside of devotion to a pet is that the day comes when it ends. She suffered with nerve damage in her back. Surgery was performed twice, and finally it was not an option any more. At age thirteen, I took Princess to the vet for the last time.

To this day, we all miss her.

# First Grandchild

We had just moved from Tokyo to London. Chapter 2 of my Simon Marketing career was beginning. After five years in Japan, I was now phasing in to the responsibility of running our London office.

Our first home was a furnished apartment in the heart of London, directly across from the park that faced Buckingham Palace. Quite a location!

Our son Kevin was still living in Japan. He and his wife were expecting their first child anytime now.

Then the phone rang. I picked it up.

"Dad, it's Kevin."

"Okay," I said calmly, "I'm going to give the phone to your mother. I want her to be the first to hear the news."

Pat listened with glee as Kevin shared with her that it's a boy, named Kyle Yuki.

After a few minutes, Pat handed the phone back to me. "Kevin," I said, then I completely lost it. I started crying and couldn't speak. It was a once-in-a-lifetime emotion, realizing that my son had a son of his own. Overwhelming joy took over my whole being.

The moment has never been duplicated.

# Broken Car Door

I like to think of myself as a logical-thinking, problem-solving adult. But then something happens that teaches me that common sense can sometimes be slow in coming.

For example, I pulled into a parking lot of a client's office on a recent Monday morning, grabbed the latch on the front door of my trusty 1999 Toyota Corolla, and it snapped. The latch would not open the door from the inside.

So I decided I had to exit the car through the passenger-side door; I accomplished this with difficulty by becoming a reluctant contortionist, maneuvering my feet and legs over the middle console and finally sliding into the passenger seat.

I ordered a replacement handle over the phone and was told I could pick it up the next day.

That evening, I returned home and had my wife come into the garage and open the car door from the outside.

The next morning, I drove to the auto supply store, called from the parking lot, and an employee came out to open the door.

The last stop in the repair journey was a drive to my mechanic in Lebanon. As I pulled into their parking lot I was about to call for someone to come out and free me from my trap—when the light bulb went off in my head! I slapped my forehead, laughed out loud, and said to myself in a giggly voice, "Hey, Jack, you dummy, just roll the window down and open the door yourself with the outside latch!"

The lesson: THINK. There is always more than one way to deal with a problem.

# What's in your DNA?

Our makeup as human beings can be a curious thing. Do we inherit traits, attitudes, and habits from the family gene pool? I'm not smart enough to answer that one, but it sure is a fun question. What role (if any) do the people on the family tree play in determining if I am partially the product of relatives who came before me?

I'm a good Catholic. Does the fact that great cousin John Joseph Cantwell became the first archbishop of Los Angeles from 1936 to 1947 mean anything? There is a high school in Los Angeles named after him. Many movie stars were parishioners who knew him personally.

I love to act as a creative outlet. In the last two years I had a ball playing two classic roles in our local Lebanon Community Theater. I was the Wizard in the *Wizard of Oz* (2014) and Clarence the Angel in *It's a Wonderful Life* (2015).

I've been acting on occasion since high school. I'll skip the details, but there was wonderful recognition, satisfaction, and fun all along the way. Does the fact that my namesake John "Johnny" Cantwell and his wife and stage partner Reta Walker trod the boards with their vaudeville act in the era from 1910 to 1920? Uncle John played the Palace on Broadway. He was a close friend of the famous George M. Cohan, and played Cohan roles in road productions of Cohan musicals.

My mother's father Joseph McDonald instilled in me the will to work hard and keep learning every day. Grandfather McDonald had an eighth grade education, got a job on a New York City garbage truck, then kept studying and passing civil service exams until he became the Commissioner of Sanitation of Staten Island, New York, during Fiorello LaGuardia's reign as Mayor of the Big Apple.

I love baseball. I've been a student of the game all my life. My early team, the Dodgers, abandoned Brooklyn and moved to Los Angeles in the late 1950s. My team since the seventies is the Boston Red Sox. My family tree is full of baseball lovers. One of them, distant cousin Joseph McDonald, was the General Manager of the New York Mets from 1974 to 1978.

Many of the men in my family tree could be categorized as self-made. They married good women of deep faith. I followed suit. My wife, Patricia, and I celebrated our fifty-fifth wedding anniversary on April 15, 2016. With the help of the GI Bill, my own earnings, and a bit of help from my parents, I became the first college graduate in the family (with the possible exception of Archbishop Cantwell). I'm proud of that.

So let me conclude this backstory where I began: what's in your DNA?

## Parting Remarks

Thanks for taking the time to share in my life's journey "in bits and pieces". I hope you enjoyed the read, and most importantly, I hope something you read here triggered some memories from your own life.

The book has been a labor of love for me. I started writing on scraps of paper and tucking them away in a file folder, until I finally emptied the folder and typed the contents into a word file.

My friend, graphic artist Kenn Kreiser, reviewed the word document …then we organized it into the "two per page with keywords" format that you just experienced. The original 28 pager turned into the book you just read. The original title (Jack's Haiku-inspired A Ha Moments) changed as well. I've been writing the new entries and the Backstories on and off for the past two-plus years.

During that time I met Frank Ryan. I had heard about his walk across America and contacted him for an interview. I write and edit front page community news stores for the Merchandiser here in Central Pa (one of my marketing clients) I also supervise a team of freelance writers for the publication.

Anyhow, that first meeting with Frank turned into an ongoing friendship.

We meet socially for breakfast every few weeks. Frank shared his book (Life Lessons Learned) with me, and subsequently introduced me to his publisher, Xlibris.

The rest, as you can see, is history.

Thanks for this special opportunity to share with you.

God bless!

Printed in the United States
By Bookmasters